PIERCE YOUR NIPPLES, SAVE YOUR SOUL

I0459728

Samdi Ajangri

Ajangri in Words | WSeditions
Philadelphia, PA

Cover Design by Ivy Desire
Edited by DC Thomas

Samdi Ajangri
Philadelphia, PA
www.ajangri.me

Pierce Your Nipples, Save Your Soul/Samdi Ajangri. -- 1st ed.
ISBN 978-1-957112-12-1

To all the past versions of Samdi who've coalesced into this one—you turned out okay, kid.

Contents

A Quick Editor's Note 1

An Author's Introduction 3

1:27 am 5

learned things 7

apple tree blooms 8

dying men 10

who you built the house for 12

find your mother, let her go 15

dead men 17

when democracy needs us all 19

anger 21

gender studies 23

pierce your nipples, save your soul 26

cohesion, a body in process 27

an arrival 28

A Quick Editor's Note

"Fuck what they think. Take up space. Y'know, let 'em wait." - Oswald Cobblepot, *The Penguin*

Nothing about Samdi Ajangri betrayed the fact they were disabled when we began talking over the dating app where we encountered each other. They took up as much space as everyone else, a few megabytes of memory and data, the same 2x5 or so inches of screen space. Nothing about Samdi Ajangri betrayed the expanse within them. We lamented the destruction of the Library of Alexandria (I'll see you in March, Caesar). We planned on holding hands a lot. They had a lot to say all the time. How could one person contain such multitudes? How many lives can a person live?

It turns out Samdi Ajangri is a multitude of lives waiting to be held in other hands. Samdi is history and possibility, an impossibly complex web of calamity and conspiracy and cool and consequence and other words that probably start with 'c' and are related to agency and being interesting.

Samdi doesn't speak for all disabled people or all queer people or all people with complicated feelings about their mother, but they're really good at speaking for themself.

1

They stutter. Their mouth muscles move at the mercy of their cerebral palsy, but the words in this chapbook are at the mercy of Samdi because Samdi can do that to words on pages and also through their stutter.

This chapbook is Samdi taking up space. Hold a little bit of them in this chapbook in your hands. Be at the mercy of them.

An Author's Introduction

I'm not gonna hold you, dear reader: 2024 was really fucking rough. I left a relatively well-paying job because it increasingly made me feel as if my soul was trying to tear itself away from my body, and that set off a lot of panic over finances and finding another source of income and whether or not I would have to consider moving back in with my parents at some point if/when I can no longer afford rent. Rent, mind you, for an unfinished apartment in which the ceiling leaked twice in the span of a month over the summer.

There was also the election. Which made me angry and scared in a way I don't think I've ever felt before. It was made all the worse when I kept hearing from my family of immigrants that I "shouldn't worry" about all that actually, because laws exist and rights exist, but history, actually, doesn't exist. Fascism isn't a documented historical fact with clear indicators apparently.

But despite those bad, terrifying, infuriating things, among many other things, I have a hard time saying I wasn't also really happy. In quitting my job, I found I had more free time. And in this free time, I found myself going outside. And, surprisingly, I didn't hate it?

My partner took me to a small community farm near where they live, and going there became a weekly routine until it got too cold and the plants got too dead. I also started volunteering at a bookstore, which has made me believe in community again—the good kind! My partner also took me out on dates! Movies! Magic horny gardens! A haunted house!

I got in back in touch with my creativity. I launched a freelance editing business, I published a couple of essays, and I rediscovered my passion for graphic design.

Perhaps most relevantly, out of all that came this little collection, which documents a lot of the emotions I grappled with. A couple of these poems, "gender studies" and "who you built the house for," were written a few years ago, but I felt they fit in well here.

2024 was incredibly difficult, but it was a year where I fell in love and grew and learned I was capable of growing. I learned what I was capable of handling and doing. I learned transformation. I learned friendship and care. It was a beautiful year, and I welcome you, dear reader, into this capsule of such a year.

1:27 am

catastrophe awaits here,
in the wee hours of the morning,
trapped between your mistakes
and the bills you don't have money to pay
and the home you cannot return to

and you were unhappy, yes, but
and you wanted to die, yes, but
and your brain wanted to give in

yes, but

your meltdowns were growing acidic,
dread grey-shading your sundays,
muted on calls releasing screams
you feared might split you in half
or reduce you to dust

in forced conversations about nothing
because those people knew nothing,
but they refused to admit it

you could've stuck it out
and just killed yourself a different way,
drown yourself in the anger,
or boil yourself alive as it rose

what's the recipe for combustion

does it even matter now

you have arrived at catastrophe
and cannot shut your eyes,
stuck between the meals you skip
and the tears you've exhausted

learned things

disabusing myself of the notion
that i should not, under any circumstances,
trust the dishwasher to do what my hands can,
or save me water, or save me time,
or spare me dysfunction-spirals
or the exhaustion pooling around my joints,
or use it as anything other than other storage

habits die hard, they say,
time-honored machine distrust passed down
and in the process of killing, i discover
i am not allergic to the sun, and a bus ride
across the city to south philly
won't kill me

and saying "i love you" first?
or trailing it behind your tongue?
couch it as a joke if they don't feel it
i mean, they like your humor
and they fucked you this morning
now, presently where you perch,
with your heart cracked open,
study their face, where sincerity
must've originated, first gathered,
in this moment you'd swear—
breathe in, and find yourself still capable
breathe out, and find it didn't end you

apple tree blooms

sentimentality maligned,
vulnerability makes me ill.
but this evening,
i brought up our little forming thing,
and how much i value clarity
and intention,
and you mentioned how you wanted
to reframe growth, how
you didn't want to think of relationships
as built, but growing.

and you want to do away with transaction
and capitalists spewing grindset
and economic ad infinitums,
all the ways they could spill
into our intimacy,
unhealthy, leading to festation, boiling blood—
no, not that type of growth.

instead you want organic,
an alive thing, fostered,
part of an ecosystem,
apple trees growing in forests
where the environment is conducive
to doing so,
seedlings nurtured in tempered soil,
with ample room to spread and stretch,
and time and care,
watered enough, undroughted.

and, fuck, bro, i'm already in love with you,
so here i am making myself sick,
doing the vulnerable-sentimental,
writing poetry that's unspecial, too sugary,
because flowers are such a tired topic,
made too evergreen by centuries
of comparison and collection and study.

here i am anyway,
more than happy to sit with you,
watching as the apple blossoms bloom,
as they take shape, in the clarity of you,
as they float and dance in the wind,
as they fill the open air with sweetness.

sit here sometime
and watch with me, please,
as the petals sprout out of my skin.

dying men

men who taught me
my body wasn't mine,
who ingrained their power
into me, over me,
eyeing me into oblivion,
touching me into a void

those men,
they are dying,
and i would like to revel,
because i used to think death
would become them,
sweet, bitter, beautiful discomfort
would be their karma,
and relief would release me,
set me soaring free,
a tear-jerking thing

but now these men are dying,
and i don't even have words,
i am left without words,
i am not allowed words,
and what good would it do
if they have lost all memory

and nobody else remembers
because they are too busy
figuring out when
they should start mourning

when nobody else
wants to remember

who you built the house for

when you grew up, you became a police
officer
you told me the story of your teeth,
nearly mythic, chipped chasing legend,
how you earned your spine and breath

i don't see you smile anymore
i can't look you in the face anymore
so i don't try

when you grew up, thunder carried you away
you told me the story of your parents,
beat down and beating down heavier,
or the stories of your foundation

what a structure you had,
drilled in, nailed in, leveled out, toughened
down
the material rotted through

when you grew up, you welcomed me in
you told me the story of my birth,
a miracle, you said, a prayer handed off,
or the stories of the almost-deaths

and i didn't ask for this,
but you told me i needed to fight for this—
my shock when the worst would be against
you

and when you grew older, you bought a house,
promised a dream,
utterings of love and air, infinite, unconditional

you fixed up a house, declared it a home,
and used my body as a doorstop,
my head as a hammer

you wanted better, whatever you had to do,
but better always meant pride
and pride means you're never wrong

and abuse begets abuse
you know this

pain breeds pain
you know this

and blood can draw blood
you know this

flesh rearing up, your teeth
won't stop if left unchecked
but you already know this

crumbling the world around you,
until you have nothing left but the house,
until there's nothing but the shadow,
until you can only breathe out dust

say it again, say "i love you" again
oh, yell it, pour it out
shed the lining of your lungs for it

break apart for it, split
right down the middle for it
shatter, atom by a t o m

maybe you'll find the meaning of it
and maybe you'll finally mean it

until you have nothing left

find your mother, let her go

in between

the silence of watching your husband
use my head to test the strength
of a porch pillar,
pleas on his behalf
for forgiveness i'll never owe,
pleas for me to apologize
for the shattering of me,
the refusal to remember
a name i use to find the pieces
of me and ease them back together,
and *i wonder if that's why he left you*

once,
i thought you the same as me
a victim, worn tired and teary,
and i could still convince you
we could free ourselves and flee,
grab my brothers' hands,
and begin again beyond terror,
taste more than survival

talking was all we'd need,
a plan of action to a running start

and i waited

in between a father and a miracle,
a house and a garden,

a promise and forever,
love and a husband,
a child and your husband,
your child and a husband

dead men

what do you do when you can't
bring yourself to care,
if you've tried to shed tears
or scream at the universe
but you've arrived at this,
the cold distance

and all you know you'll do
at the funeral is try not to laugh,
bitter and hot and sharp,
biting it down, back,
a single loud, ugly cackle
fought back
into your chest,
hysterics
threatening to blossom or erupt,
you're unsure which,
from your chest

your chest you were told
wasn't yours
and out of respect for your elders
you shouldn't hide
or try to move away
or try to brush the hand away
or even ever
breathe out in discomfort

what do you do
who do you tell

what do you say
what can you say

is it selfish
if you can't bring yourself
to mourn with the others?

when democracy needs us all

noble-sounding calls for keeping
democracy in tact every four years,
silicon coating your dollar bills,
silicon transforming your hands,
silicon down your throat

some rideshare company notifies me:
voters get 35% off
on rides to the polls

as i'm paving america
with my blood and tears and taxes
between infinity in underfunded
bureaucracy and noncitizenship
and terror loops through legality

democracy is far-off places
hungry men see as interchangeable
battleground-graves,
imperial land for the taking
where only insects exist

and half an island forced
into never-ending orbit
around western sun
could sink into the ocean
and it wouldn't make a difference

and after you hollow out solidarity
and wear your bare minimum loud,

you tell me sorry,
normalcy was your only option

anger

anger in my chest
anger that swells
anger that has no home

anger that swallows me
anger i swallow back
anger that chokes me
anger i cannot talk out

anger mean and menacing
anger at the world
anger at my body
anger when my eyes crack open

anger that turns me helpless,
    a crying, sobbing, heaving thing,
    a screaming, anxious, little thing

anger joining hands with despair
    until i decide
    it must be put to better use

anger i cannot hold
anger i must
anger becoming my bones,
    setting me upright,
    my blood on fire

anger my anchor
anger my hope

anger my clarity

anger my ancestor

anger to tear down
anger to build anew
anger to set us free

gender studies

monday, my gender is the violence
i've been told to swallow, acid
forced down my throat, violation
and you don't know what's good for you
and you need to be corrected
and you're just trying to get hit,
aren't you?
aren't you?
well, am i?

tuesday i remember a photo,
edges time-softened, from a book
spanning lives and experiments
and histories i can't fathom,
that tells me my gender is "colored,"
because proper restrooms and by extension
the labels "men" and "women"
are reserved for humans

wednesday is the day i'm slammed
back into memory
because sex for me is memory
and i try to make sense of what happened
when i was too little
to hold words on my tongue,
whatever sense one can make, years later,
after you've buried it away,
when it happens again and again,
carving you out, caving me in,
and my conclusion is that i don't know

and analysis won't help

anyway, my gender on thursday is recognizing
that humanity is also denied
when superhumanity is granted,
or it's thrust upon you,
heavy and folded, your back folding,
with no choice but to never break
because you can't, they won't let you
and softness isn't allowed
and maybe you save everyone else,
but who saves you?

on friday, my gender is paradox
because the nigger is outside of genre
or category or type or—
and the slave is outside of time, and space,
and science can attempt to explain
the physiology of pain,
but it can't explain the heaviness,
and the way it sticks and follows
or the way it stretches or—
but the nigger woman is still asked
to perform like she'll one day be lauded

and on saturday, i am nothing
but the void and the spiral,
canceled out by contradiction,
making friends with them both
intimacy is mine in here, only mine,
and i lay claim to rest

sunday, my gender is everything beyond me,

ahead of me, behind me,
the history of colors and emptiness
shapeless now, rising, creating myself
in a freedom that exists
outside of care and comfort,
i shed, become new
and a lover once said i'm divine,
and this day i'm inclined to believe them

pierce your nipples, save your soul

i can't wait for the summer
when i can retire my bras
and wear bravery,
tight and form-fitting, instead

cohesion, a body in process

hypervigilant of defect,
i find myself looking away
from glass windows
when i walk down the street

my jaw clicks when i open my mouth
to yawn because i once decided
relocating it myself
was easier than panicking
my parents awake

but you've thanked me
for being pretty as hell,
and you enjoy discovering
new ways to enjoy me

where modification adds color,
where piercing means control,
where we fold and become art

so allowing me to melt
on your tongue
won't cure me,
but it does come
impossibly close

an arrival

you asked me to write about the happy
i hope for, but i simply can't imagine
a future happy where i am not held
in your arms

i've tried to not be so sentimental
or sound twee

but you told me to work with the intensity
because i'd always end up choking
on attempts to keep it down,
and something thawed then, a new thing
took shape, was set free

and happy is within city limits,
but, god, this city is huge

a bus ride isn't going to kill me,
and i found a garden i can tend
without memory of contempt,
and a bookstore can be more
than the building and its inventory

a future happy is more and more days
discovering what lies
in the heat of summer,
when you're in bloom
and you take my hand

more and more days

when it's colder and quieter,
spent with hot chocolate,
and adventure is in the blankets,
and i'm only ever warm enough
when you kiss me

ABOUT THE AUTHOR

Samdi Ajangri is a Haitian-born, American-raised resident who does hard things like walking along uneven floors without falling, writing (and editing) words and creating things, and being in community with people who can be a little annoying sometimes. They think these hard things are worth doing. They live in Philadelphia, PA with their two gremlin-cats, Pentha and Bast.

Visit Samdi online at ajangri.me.